Heartwise

Cultivating Emotional Intelligence for Teens

Journal

Teen Edition

Iyla Joshu

A Note from the Author

This book was created using a combination of AI assistance and human editing. I used artificial intelligence as a tool to help shape, draft, and organize the ideas presented here—but every word has been reviewed, reworked, and refined by me to ensure that the voice, message, and meaning align with my values and lived experience.

In the spirit of transparency and integrity—which are core themes of this work—I believe it's important to share this. The result is a collaboration between human insight and modern tools, crafted with care and a clear moral compass.

Because how we make things matters just as much as what we make.

Table of Contents

Introduction

In "Heartwise Journal– Cultivating Emotional Intelligence for Teens," we'll embark on a journey to discover the transformative power of emotional intelligence. Each chapter builds upon the last, guiding you from the foundations of self-awareness to the practical application of EQ in your daily life. This journal follows the book, "Heartwise – Cultivating Emotional Intelligence for Teens, Teen Edition" and is filled with interactive exercises that will help you create an in-depth understanding of your emotions and those of others.

This journal provides a space for practicing actionable strategies and can help you find real-world insights. As a teen, you face many challenges, from academic stress to peer pressure. Emotional intelligence is the key to thriving during this time. By growing your EQ, you'll build resilience, strengthen your relationships, and gain a profound sense of self-understanding.

Throughout the journal, you'll find the interactive elements discussed in the book which are designed to help you personalize your learning experience. From worksheets to thought prompts, these tools will encourage you to think about your own emotions and experiences, making the concepts come alive in a way that resonates with you.

A journal can reveal patterns in your experiences, helping you identify personal strengths and areas for improvement. As you review past entries, you might notice recurring themes or challenges, offering clues about your emotional triggers and responses. This awareness allows you to make intentional adjustments, enhancing your ability to work through similar situations in the future. Furthermore, documenting your achievements, no matter how small, fosters a sense of accomplishment and motivation. Celebrating these milestones reinforces your resilience, affirming that each step forward, even in the face of adversity, is a victory worth acknowledging.

By the end of this journey, you'll have gained a toolbox of practical strategies for managing your emotions, communicating effectively, and cultivating empathy. You'll be equipped with the skills to handle even the toughest challenges, from acing that big presentation to navigating complex social situations.

So, are you ready to embark on this life-changing journey? To discover the incredible power that lies within you? Then, let's dive in together and unlock the skills that will help you find success in the face of any emotional challenge that comes your way.

Chapter 1:
Understanding Yourself

If you've ever felt like emotions are controlling your life, you're not alone. Understanding yourself is the first step to gaining control over these feelings and transforming how you interact with the world.

1.1 Emotional Clarity: Recognizing What You Feel

Recognizing and labeling emotions accurately is the cornerstone of emotional intelligence. Developing an emotional vocabulary is your first step. Words like "frustrated," "overwhelmed," or "content" allow you to precisely express what you're feeling. This precision is important because it allows you to address the core of your emotions rather than getting lost in bunch of basic feelings that don't express how you really feel.

Here is a list of 50 emotions and their definitions to start your journey:
Adventurous – Wanting to try new things and take risks
Angry – Frustrated or upset about something
Annoyed – Bothered by something or someone
Ashamed – Feeling bad about something done or said
Betrayed – Hurt by someone breaking trust
Bored – Not interested in anything at the moment
Calm – Feeling peaceful and at ease
Confident – Feeling sure of oneself and abilities
Confused – Not sure what to think or feel
Connected – Feeling close to friends, family, or a group
Curious – Wanting to learn or explore

Defensive – Feeling the need to protect oneself from criticism
Defeated – Feeling like giving up
Disappointed – Let down by an outcome
Eager – Excited and ready to do something
Embarrassed – Feeling self-conscious or awkward
Empathetic – Understanding and sharing others' emotions
Excited – Eager or looking forward to something
Frustrated – Feeling stuck or unable to achieve something
Grateful – Appreciative of what you have
Guilty – Regretting an action or decision
Happy – Feeling joyful or content
Helpless – Feeling like nothing can be done to fix a situation
Hopeful – Expecting good things to happen
Hopeless – Feeling like things won't improve
Independent – Wanting to make choices without help
Insecure – Doubting oneself or feeling not good enough
Inspired – Motivated by something or someone
Jealous – Wanting what someone else has
Judged – Feeling criticized by others
Lonely – Feeling isolated or disconnected
Loved – Feeling cared for and valued
Mischievous – Playfully causing trouble or bending rules
Motivated – Ready to take action and work toward goals
Nervous – Feeling anxious about something upcoming
Optimistic – Expecting good things to happen
Overwhelmed – Too much to handle at once
Pressured – Feeling pushed to meet expectations
Proud – Feeling accomplished or successful
Regretful – Wishing something had been done differently
Rejected – Feeling unwanted or excluded
Relieved – Feeling at ease after stress is gone
Resentful – Holding onto anger about something unfair
Restless – Unable to sit still or focus
Sad – Feeling down or low
Scared – Afraid of something happening
Shy – Feeling nervous around people or in social settings
Stressed – Pressured by school, friends, or expectations
Unappreciated – Feeling like efforts go unnoticed
Worried – Concerned about what might happen

Emotions don't just come out of thin air; they have triggers. By identifying these triggers, you are able to piece together the clues that lead to your emotional responses.

Start by asking yourself simple yet profound questions:

- "What am I feeling right now?"
- "Why did that make me so upset?"
- "What thoughts are connected to this feeling?"
- "Have I felt this way before?
  - When?"

Journaling can be an invaluable tool here. When you write down prompts like:

- "When I feel [emotion], I tend to...,"
- "What can I do to handle this feeling in a healthy way?"
- "How is this emotion affecting my thoughts and actions?"

You're not just recording your thoughts; you're analyzing them, seeking patterns that reveal your inner workings.

Use this space to write down your thoughts and responses.

_____

_____

_____

_____

_____

_____

_____

_____

_____

_____

_____

_____

_____

_____

1.2 The Mood Journal: Track Your Emotional Patterns

Thinking on prompts can deepen your journaling experience, encouraging you to explore the underlying causes of your emotions. Ask yourself:

- "What events led to this mood?"
- "Is this feeling connected to a specific person, event, or thought?"
- "Am I reacting to the present moment, or is this emotion influenced by past experiences?"
- "Have I felt this way before in similar situations?"

A journal entry might look like this:

Date	What Happened?	How I Felt (words or emojis)	What Helped Me Feel Better?
5/10	Failed my quiz	😦 frustrated, disappointed	Talked to a friend, went for a walk

Use this space to explore your thoughts and responses.

_____

_____

_____

_____

_____

_____

_____

_____

_____

_____

_____

_____

1.3 Inside Out: How Emotions Affect Your Body

Understanding how emotions affect your body is a fundamental aspect of emotional intelligence. By recognizing the physical signals your body sends, you can take proactive steps to manage your emotional health. This awareness enhances your ability to cope with stress and improves your quality of life, allowing you to experience emotions in a fuller and healthier way.

Ask yourself:
- What events led to these physical feelings?
- What steps can I take to manage my emotions to prevent these physical feelings?

Use this space to write down your thoughts and responses.

_____

_____

_____

_____

_____

_____

_____

_____

_____

_____

_____

_____

_____

_____

_____

_____

Tiny space for tiny doodles

1.5 The Power of Self-Talk: Transform Your Inner Dialogue

When you speak to yourself, what do you hear? This internal dialogue, known as self-talk, can shape your emotions and actions in profound ways. It's the personal conversation that runs through your mind, influencing how you perceive challenges and celebrating victories. Think of it as the narrator of your life story.

Self-reflection is a powerful tool in this process. By engaging in exercises designed to increase awareness of your self-talk patterns, you can identify areas for improvement. Use journal prompts to explore your internal dialogue deeply.

Self-Talk Journal Prompts
Questions like these encourage introspection and growth:
- "What negative thoughts do I notice repeating?"
- "How can I reframe these into positive affirmations?"

Use this space to write down your thoughts and responses.

_____

_____

_____

_____

_____

_____

_____

_____

_____

_____

_____

Space for doodles

Chapter 2:
Emotional Regulation Techniques

When you breathe deeply, your body receives more oxygen, which calms your nervous system. The immediate effect is a reduction in anxiety and a sense of tranquility. It's like flipping a switch that tells your body it's okay to relax, even when stress is high. This simple act of focusing on your breath can quiet the chaos in your mind, laying the groundwork for clearer thinking and emotional balance.

To harness the power of breathwork, let's explore a couple of techniques. The 4-7-8 breathing technique is a popular exercise that can be your go-to in stressful moments. Start by inhaling quietly through your nose for a count of four. Hold your breath for a count of seven. Then, exhale completely through your mouth for a count of eight. This rhythmic pattern calms your mind and slows your heart rate, making it a perfect tool for immediate stress relief. Another helpful method is box breathing, which involves inhaling for four counts, holding the breath for four counts, exhaling for four counts, and then pausing for four counts before the next inhale. This technique is favored by athletes and performers who need to maintain composure under pressure, and it can be equally beneficial for you in daily life.

In practical terms, think of breath work as your emotional first-aid kit, ready to be deployed in various situations. Before a big test or presentation, take a few moments to practice the 4-7-8 technique. It helps to center your thoughts and ease the anxiety that might otherwise cloud your performance. During a heated conflict with a friend or family member, box breathing can provide the pause necessary to collect your thoughts and respond thoughtfully rather than reactively. These techniques empower you to face immediate stressors and build your resilience over time, equipping you with a lifelong skill for emotional balance.

Breathing Exercise Checklist
- **4-7-8 Technique:** Inhale (4), Hold (7), Exhale (8)
- **Box Breathing:** Inhale (4), Hold (4), Exhale (4), Pause (4)

Breathwork reminds you that you possess a natural, powerful tool to work through life's emotional ups and downs. By integrating these techniques into your routine, you can transform moments of tension into opportunities for calm and clarity. Whether you're in the classroom, at home, or facing unexpected challenges, remember that the power to change how you feel is just a breath away.

Choose one of these techniques and practice it 3 times a day for a week to help it become part of your daily life. Check off each time you practice.

Day 1	Day 2	Day 3	Day 4	Day 5	Day 6	Day 7

2.1 The Mindful Minute: Quick Stress Relievers

Mindfulness is the practice of being nonjudgmental and aware of your thoughts and emotions. Micro-mindfulness can help you find pockets of peace amidst the hustle and bustle. Micro-mindfulness involves incorporating brief, intentional moments of awareness into your daily routine. It's about being fully present, even if just for a minute, and allowing that presence to transform mundane tasks into opportunities for tranquility and clarity.

Bringing mindfulness into your busy schedule doesn't require drastic changes. Set reminders on your phone to prompt you to take mindful pauses throughout the day. Pair mindfulness with existing routines, like eating lunch. As you eat, savor each bite, noting the flavors and textures. This intentional practice enhances enjoyment and trains your mind to stay present. These small, consistent practices weave mindfulness into the fabric of your life, offering stability amidst the ever-changing demands of adolescence.

Mindfulness Reminder Tips
- Set phone alarms for daily mindful minutes
- Link mindfulness to tasks like eating or commuting

Embracing the mindful minute transforms the way you experience the world. It's a reminder that you have the power to create calm and focus, no matter how hectic life gets. Each moment of mindfulness is a step toward greater emotional balance and well-being.

Find ways to bring micro-mindfulness into your daily routine and practice it 3 times a day for a week to help it become part of your daily life. Check off each time you practice.

Day 1	Day 2	Day 3	Day 4	Day 5	Day 6	Day 7

2.2 Emotional First Aid Kit: Handling Overwhelming Feelings

Picture a day when emotions hit like a tidal wave—unexpected and overpowering. Early intervention is key; just as you wouldn't wait for a small cut to become infected before treating it, addressing emotional distress promptly can prevent it from escalating. These quick-access tools are your frontline defense against emotional turmoil, providing relief and clarity when you need it most.

Building your emotional first aid kit starts with identifying what soothes you. Music is a powerful ally in this endeavor. Create playlists filled with your favorite calming songs—those tracks that, when the first notes play, instantly transport you to a place of peace. Alongside your auditory aids, consider physical objects like stress balls or fidget spinners.

Self-compassion is another vital component of your toolkit. When emotions run high, it's easy to fall into the trap of self-criticism, but this only makes the situation more difficult. Instead, practice self-kindness. Writing a letter to yourself can be a powerful act of self-compassion. In this letter, acknowledge your feelings, express understanding, and offer words of encouragement as if you were speaking to a close friend. Similarly, positive self-affirmations serve as a counterbalance to negative self-talk. Phrases like "I am worthy" or "I am doing my best" can become mantras that ground you during turbulent times. These affirmations, repeated regularly, help rewire your brain to default to positivity rather than self-doubt.

Creating a personalized emotional first-aid kit requires introspection and honesty.
- Start by journaling about your personal triggers.
  - Are there specific situations or interactions that consistently create strong emotional responses?
  - By identifying these, you can prepare strategies and tools tailored to your unique needs.
- Consider which coping mechanisms have been helpful in the past.
  - Was it a particular song, a walk in nature, or maybe a phone call with a supportive friend?

Incorporate these elements into your kit, knowing they've proven helpful before. This personalization ensures that your emotional first aid kit is a carefully curated set of resources that resonate with you.

11

Emotional First Aid Kit Checklist

- Calming Music Playlist: Add your favorite songs that soothe your mind.
- Stress-Relief Objects: Include items like stress balls or fidget spinners.
- Self-Compassion Tools: Prepare to write self-compassionate letters and affirmations.
- Journal for Triggers: Identify situations that trigger strong emotions and coping strategies that work well for you.

Use this space to write down personal triggers, coping mechanisms that have worked, compassionate messages to yourself and any other ideas you find to have at hand.

_____

_____

_____

_____

_____

_____

_____

_____

_____

_____

_____

_____

_____

_____

Space for doodles

2.3 Running on Empty: Understanding Emotional Bankruptcy

But what happens when emotional overwhelm becomes the norm—when you've spent so long managing stress that you're running on fumes? That's when we step into the deeper territory of emotional bankruptcy.

Sometimes, it's not just that you're having a bad day — it's that you've hit emotional bankruptcy.

Think of your emotions like a bank account. Every time you deal with stress, help someone else, hold in your feelings, or pretend you're fine when you're not... you're spending emotional energy. If you keep withdrawing without putting anything back in — rest, support, boundaries, or time to breathe — eventually, you're broke.

That's emotional bankruptcy: when you feel numb, exhausted, snappy, or like you just don't care anymore. You're not lazy. You're drained.

The fix? You need deposits. That means:

- Saying no.
- Resting without guilt.
- Asking for help.
- Doing stuff that fills you up (even if it's just a walk, music, or saying "no thanks" to drama)

You don't have to hit zero before you recharge. Start noticing when your emotional balance is dipping low — and take care of it like it matters. Because it does.

Have you ever experienced emotional bankruptcy? What happened that got you to that point?

_____

_____

_____

_____

_____

_____

_____

_____

_____

_____

_____

_____

_____

_____

_____

_____

_____

What do you think you can do in the future to recognize you are headed there?

_____

_____

_____

_____

_____

_____

_____

What activities fill you up?

_____

_____

_____

_____

_____

_____

_____

_____

_____

_____

Space for doodles

2.4 Turning the Tide: Shifting from Negative to Positive Emotions

Imagine a time when a setback made you feel like the world was crashing down. These moments, often stinging with failure, can seem insurmountable. Yet, what if you could change your perspective, viewing these setbacks not as insurmountable barriers but as stepping stones for growth? This is where cognitive reframing steps in, offering a new lens through which to see challenges.

To practice reframing, start with thought replacement charts. These tools allow you to identify negative thoughts and consciously replace them with positive ones. Draw a line down the middle of a page. On one side, write down a negative thought. On the opposite side, brainstorm a positive or neutral alternative. For example, "I'll never understand this subject" might become "I'm improving every day with practice." This exercise encourages flexibility in thinking and helps you recognize the patterns that may be holding you back. Another helpful tool is gratitude exercises, especially during tough times. By focusing on what you are grateful for, even when things seem bleak, you can shift your mindset from one of scarcity to one of abundance. Maybe it's the unwavering support of a friend or the comfort of a favorite book. Acknowledging these positives can lighten the weight of negative experiences, fostering a sense of inner strength and hope.

Here is a sample chart:

Negative Thought	New Positive or Neutral Thought
"I'm terrible at this."	"I'm still learning, and that's okay."
"Nobody likes me."	"I have friends who care about me."

Create your own list to refer to until this process becomes a habit:

Negative thought   **New Positive or Neutral alternative**

_____   _____

_____   _____

_____   _____

_____   _____

_____   _____

_____   _____

_____   _____

_____   _____

_____   _____

_____   _____

_____   _____

_____   _____

_____   _____

_____   _____

Space for Doodles

2.5 The Art of Letting Go: Release and Move Forward

Vision Board Creation Steps

The base of the Vision Board:
- Get a sheet of poster board or cardboard to arrange your images and words on.
- Gather Materials: Find magazines, photos, and words that resonate with your goals.
- Arrange with Intention: Place your images and words on the board in a way that inspires you.
- Display Prominently: Keep your vision board in a place where you'll see it daily'

These practices of letting go, forgiveness, and focusing on future goals are central to emotional well-being. They empower you to release what no longer serves you and to embrace the present with openness and hope.

Big Space for Doodles and Ideas

Chapter 3:
Building Empathy and Understanding

Empathy is not just about feeling sorry for someone, which is sympathy; it's about genuinely stepping into their shoes and experiencing the world from their perspective.

The benefits of empathy extend far beyond individual connections. Empathy acts as a glue in relationships, binding people together through understanding and compassion. When you empathize with someone, you're acknowledging their emotional experience and validating it.

Reflecting on empathy experiences can deepen your understanding and growth. Daily empathy reflections are a powerful tool for cultivating this skill. At the end of each day, take a moment to consider a situation where you practiced empathy or could have done so. Think about the emotions involved and the effect your empathy had on the interaction.

Empathy is a skill that enriches your life and the lives of those around you. It reminds us that, at our core, we all seek understanding and connection. By nurturing empathy, you enhance your relationships and contribute to a world where compassion and kindness reign.

Empathy Reflection Journal Prompt Ideas
- Think about a situation today where you practiced empathy.
- What did you learn about the other person's perspective?
- How did it change the interaction?
- What mix of feelings do I have now that I understand a new perspective?

Use this space to write down your thoughts and responses.

3.1 The Empathy Map: Understanding Perspectives

An empathy map is a tool that helps you deal with the complex terrain of human emotions and perspectives, providing clarity and direction. It helps you visualize what others think, feel, say, and do, allowing you to create a fuller picture of their experience. By mapping out these dimensions, you identify common ground and recognize the nuances of their journey. This visualization fosters a deeper understanding, making it easier to relate to and connect with others.

Empathy Map Creation Steps

EMPATHY MAP

SAY	DO
"I'm fine"	Looks down, avoids eye contact
FEEL	**THINK**
Maybe sad or stressed	"No one gets how I feel."

- Divide a sheet of paper into four sections:
  - 'What they say,' '
  - What they do,'
  - 'What they feel,'
  - 'What they think.'
- Observe conversations for recurring themes.
- Note their actions and behaviors.
- Intuit emotions and potential thoughts.
- Apply insights to resolve conflicts and improve relationships.

Empathy maps are not just tools; they're bridges that connect us to others, fostering understanding in a world where miscommunication often reigns. By using them, you equip yourself with a powerful resource for empathy.

Practice Empathy Maps

SAY	DO
FEEL	THINK

SAY	DO
FEEL	THINK

SAY	DO
FEEL	THINK

SAY	DO
FEEL	THINK

3.2 Listening Like a Pro: Active Listening Skills

Listening, especially active listening, is a conscious effort to truly understand the speaker, not just by their words but also by their emotions and intentions. It involves entirely focusing, understanding, responding, and remembering what was said. This kind of listening builds trust, showing someone their thoughts and feelings are valued. It's the foundation of meaningful relationships, where communication flows openly and honestly.

To practice active listening, start with reflective listening exercises. When someone shares something, reflect back what you heard. This doesn't mean parroting their words but summarizing the essence of their message. For example, if a friend says they're stressed about exams, you might respond, "Wow, that sounds really hard. I totally get it — school stress hits me like that too." This reflection shows that you're listening and gives the speaker a chance to clarify or expand on their thoughts. Paraphrasing and summarizing are key skills here. They involve restating what you heard in your own words, like capturing the main points of a conversation in a brief summary. This helps both parties ensure understanding and keeps the dialogue productive and supportive.

Despite its benefits, active listening faces several barriers. Distractions are the most common. Whether it's a buzzing phone or a wandering mind, these interruptions can derail attentive listening. To overcome this, create a distraction-free environment by silencing notifications or choosing a quiet place to talk. Another challenge is managing internal biases. These are the preconceived notions and judgments we bring into conversations, which can color our understanding. Being aware of these biases and setting them aside is crucial for genuine listening. Come to each conversation with an open mind, ready to accept and consider new perspectives without letting past experiences cloud your judgment.

Practice Exercise: Active Listening Role-Plays
- Pair up with a friend or family member.
- Take turns sharing a story or concern.
- Practice reflecting, paraphrasing, and summarizing the other person's message.
- Discuss the experience and any insights gained.

Active listening is more than a skill; it's a commitment to understanding and connecting with others. Try role-plays to practice. Find a partner and take turns sharing stories or concerns. As you listen, focus on reflecting, paraphrasing, and summarizing the speaker's message. This exercise not only enhances listening skills but also fosters empathy and understanding. Listening for emotions rather than words is another powerful technique. Pay attention to the speaker's tone, body language, and facial expressions. These non-verbal cues often convey more than words alone, revealing the true depth of emotion behind the message.

Practicing active listening transforms how you interact with others. It deepens relationships, fosters empathy, and creates a safe space for open dialogue. By strengthening these skills, you improve your communication and enrich your connections, building a network of trust and understanding.

Journal notes: To help you track what you struggle with and what you do well with

I did well with the following

_____

_____

_____

_____

_____

_____

_____

_____

_____

_____

_____

_____

_____

_____

_____

I could improve on

The Power of Kindness: Random Acts for Social Good

Imagine a small pebble thrown into a tranquil pond. It creates ripples that extend far beyond the point of impact, touching every corner of the water's surface. Kindness works in much the same way. A simple act, like holding the door open for someone or sharing a smile, can create waves of positivity that extend well beyond the initial gesture. In a world where negativity often seems to dominate, these ripples of kindness have the power to enact important social change.

The science behind kindness reveals its profound effect on emotional well-being. When you do acts of kindness, your brain releases chemicals like endorphins and oxytocin, often called the 'feel-good' hormones. Endorphins create a sense of happiness and fulfillment, while oxytocin enhances feelings of trust and bonding, reducing stress and anxiety. This biological response improves your mood and strengthens your immune system, proving that kindness is beneficial for both the mind and body. By understanding the science behind kindness, you gain insight into its power to transform lives, making it an essential element of emotional intelligence.

To get into the habit of doing regular acts of kindness, consider setting up kindness challenges. A kindness jar is a fun way to remind yourself to do daily acts of kindness. Fill a jar with simple acts, like "give someone a compliment" or "help a friend with homework." Each day, draw a note and complete the task, creating a routine of kindness that becomes second nature. Another idea is setting weekly kindness goals. At the beginning of each week, decide on a specific kindness goal, like volunteering for an hour or writing a letter of appreciation. These challenges make kindness a priority and provide a sense of accomplishment and joy when completed.

Kindness Challenge Ideas

Create a kindness jar with daily kindness tasks, such as "write a thank-you note" or "share a snack." Set weekly kindness goals, like volunteering or helping someone in need.

What are 5 easy to do ideas you can come up with?

1 - _____

2- _____

3- _____

4- _____

5- _____

Kindness is a powerful tool for change, capable of transforming individual lives and entire communities. By incorporating acts of kindness into your daily activities, you contribute to a more compassionate and connected world. These actions, though seemingly small, have the potential to inspire others, creating a ripple effect that spreads positivity and hope. As you show kindness, you become an agent of change, helping to build a society where empathy, understanding, and goodwill thrive.

Space for Doodles

3.3 Cultural Sensitivity: Embracing Diversity in Interactions

Cultural sensitivity plays a pivotal role in enhancing empathetic connections. Understanding someone's cultural background makes you better able to relate to their experiences and emotions.

Reflective practices are essential for becoming cultural sensitive. Journaling about cultural learning experiences can be incredibly insightful. After attending a cultural event or engaging in a discussion, take some time to jot down your thoughts. What did you learn that surprised you? How did the experience challenge your preconceptions? This reflection helps solidify your understanding and encourages ongoing growth. Group discussions on cultural perspectives are equally valuable. Gather with peers to share insights and think about your experiences. These conversations can reveal commonalities and differences, fostering a deeper appreciation for the diversity around you. They also provide an opportunity to practice listening and empathy, key components of cultural sensitivity.

Cultural sensitivity is not just about acknowledging differences but celebrating them. In an increasingly interconnected world, the ability to engage with diverse cultures is invaluable. By embracing cultural sensitivity, you enrich your interactions and contribute to a more inclusive and harmonious society. Through understanding, empathy, and appreciation, you transform diversity from a source of tension into a wellspring of strength and inspiration. As you continue exploring these themes, remember that every interaction is an opportunity to learn and grow. Each step you take toward cultural sensitivity brings you closer to a world where everyone is valued and respected for who they are.

Cultural Exchange Reflection Prompts
- How did the cultural experience change your perspective?
- What similarities did you discover between different cultures?
- How can you apply this understanding in your interactions?

Use this space to write down your thoughts.

_____

_____

_____

_____

_____

_____

_____

_____

_____

_____

_____

_____

_____

_____

_____

_____

_____

Big Space for Doodles

Chapter 4:
Navigating Social Media and Digital Life

Social media profiles act as mirrors, reflecting not just how you wish to be seen but also what you value and believe. They can amplify your best traits or exaggerate insecurities, creating a digital identity that might not fully align with who you really are.

In the quest to craft the perfect online persona, it's easy to fall into the trap of presenting a false self. The pressure to conform to trends or appear flawless can lead you to post only carefully curated moments, excluding the less glamorous parts of life. This can create a false picture of yourself that's difficult to maintain, ultimately leading to feelings of disconnection and anxiety. To avoid these pitfalls, aligning your online presence with your values is crucial. This means sharing content that resonates with you, reflects your true interests, and represents your authentic self. By doing so, you create a digital identity that feels genuine and sustainable and doesn't crumble under the weight of social expectations.

Regular self-reflection ensures that your online identity aligns with your true self. Conduct periodic audits of your social media profiles to evaluate whether the content truly represents who you are and what you stand for.

The effects of online identity on self-esteem is profound. When your digital self accurately reflects your real-life identity, it can boost your confidence and reinforce a positive self-image.

Reflective Journaling
- Think about your most recent social media post.
  - How does it reflect your true self?
  - Does it align with your personal values?
  - What emotions did posting it evoke in you?
- Think about multiple posts
  - Do you see areas where you are not being your true self?

- What were you trying to achieve when you posted these things?
- How can you become more mindful when posting to portray your authentic self?
- Do you typically post when experiencing a particular emotion?
- Is this helping you portray your authentic self?

Understanding the role of social media in shaping identity is essential for navigating digital life with confidence and authenticity. By aligning your online presence with your true self, you empower yourself to use social media as a tool for connection and self-expression while safeguarding your self-esteem and emotional well-being.

Use this space to write down your reflections.

_____

_____

_____

_____

_____

_____

_____

_____

_____

_____

_____

_____

_____

_____

_____

_____

_____

_____

Space for Doodles

Cyber-kindness: Building Positive Online Communities

At its core, cyber-kindness is about using digital platforms to foster positivity, whether through empathetic messages or supportive interactions. It's about making the online world kinder, where everyone feels valued and respected. This method is vital in combating the negativity that can sometimes overwhelm digital interactions, replacing it with encouragement and inclusivity.

To foster cyber-kindness, consider the power of creating supportive groups and forums. These digital spaces become sanctuaries where people can share their experiences, seek advice, and offer support without fear of judgment. Sharing uplifting content is another simple yet powerful way to promote positive interactions. By sharing what inspires and uplifts you, you contribute to a culture of positivity that can transform someone's day.

The effects of cyber-kindness extends beyond individual interactions, playing a major role in enhancing mental health. Positive online interactions can reduce the prevalence of bullying and harassment, creating a safer environment for everyone. When kindness becomes the norm, there's less room for negativity to take root. Moreover, engaging in cyber-kindness fosters a sense of community and belonging. Knowing you are part of a supportive network can ease feelings of isolation and anxiety, promoting emotional well-being. These digital connections become lifelines, offering comfort and companionship in both good times and bad.

When a hashtag encouraging positivity goes viral, it unites people worldwide in a shared mission to spread kindness. These campaigns often inspire thousands to participate, proving that even small acts of kindness can have a massive influence.

Cyber-kindness is not just a concept—it's a movement that invites everyone to contribute to a more compassionate digital world. By embracing kindness online, you can help build communities where everyone feels seen, heard, and supported. It's about recognizing your power to make a difference, one post, comment, and interaction at a time. The beauty of cyber-kindness lies in its simplicity and accessibility; anyone with access to the internet can participate and make a positive impact.

Cyber-kindness Action Plan
- Identify a cause or community you're passionate about.
- Create or join a supportive online group related to this interest.
- Share an uplifting post or message once a week to spread positivity.
- What are ways you can think of to promote cyber-kindness?
- How can you put these ideas into action?

Use this space for your ideas on creating cyber-kindness.

_____

_____

_____

_____

_____

_____

_____

_____

_____

_____

_____

_____

_____

_____

_____

_____

Ghosting and Blocking: Navigating Digital Boundaries

Ghosting and blocking are two digital actions that have become part of modern language, each carrying major relationship implications. Ghosting—suddenly ceasing all communication without explanation—can leave the recipient struggling with confusion and hurt. It often raises questions about self-worth and creates an emotional void as the person left behind tries to understand what happened. On the flip side, blocking serves as a boundary-setting tool. While it can signal the end of a relationship, it can also be a healthy way to protect oneself from toxic interactions. Knowing when and how to use these tools requires understanding digital boundaries and the courage to enforce them.

Setting clear boundaries in online interactions is crucial for maintaining mental health and personal integrity. Without boundaries, it's easy to feel trapped in a cycle of endless connectivity. Establishing personal guidelines for online engagement is key to preventing overwhelm. Consider what you're comfortable sharing and with whom, as well as how much time you spend online. Recognizing toxic interactions and knowing when to disengage are equally important. If a conversation consistently leaves you feeling drained or anxious, it may be time to step back or even cut ties.

Self-reflection plays a crucial role in defining and maintaining digital boundaries. Journaling about your personal experiences with digital boundaries can offer valuable insights into what works for you. Think about past interactions that felt intrusive or uncomfortable, and consider what boundaries could have prevented those feelings. Use these reflections to create a digital boundary action plan outlining specific guidelines for your online behavior and engagement. This plan can serve as a roadmap for navigating future interactions, helping you to identify when and where to draw the line. By assessing your digital limits regularly, you empower yourself to engage online in a way that respects your personal needs and values.

Understanding and implementing digital boundaries are vital skills in today's interconnected world. By recognizing the power of ghosting and blocking, you can make informed decisions about your online presence. Though sometimes challenging, these actions are tools for maintaining emotional health and ensuring that your digital life aligns with your values and needs.

Space for Doodles

Digital Boundary Reflection Exercise

- Think about a recent digital interaction that felt uncomfortable.
- What boundaries, if any, could have prevented this feeling?
- How will you apply this insight to future interactions?

Use this space to write down your thoughts.

_____

_____

_____

_____

_____

_____

_____

_____

_____

_____

_____

_____

_____

_____

_____

FOMO No More: Mastering Digital Balance

FOMO, or Fear of Missing Out, has become a common emotional experience in our hyper-connected world. Social media amplifies FOMO by constantly showcasing snapshots of others' lives, often highlighting the most exciting or enjoyable moments. For many teens, this creates a persistent sense of inadequacy or exclusion, as if everyone else lives a more fulfilling or enjoyable life. As much as technology connects us, it also fuels a cycle of comparison and envy, affecting emotional well-being.

The psychological effects of this continuous online exposure are profound, often resulting in decreased self-esteem and increased stress. It's as if the digital world never allows you to truly switch off, constantly reminding you of what you might be missing.

There are strategies to overcome FOMO and create a healthier relationship with technology.
- One way is setting specific times for social media usage.
- Engaging in offline activities and hobbies provides a tangible escape, offering fulfillment that doesn't rely on likes or comments.
- Balancing digital and offline life isn't just about avoiding FOMO; it also enhances overall well-being.
- Reducing screen time improves focus and productivity, as your attention isn't constantly divided between notifications and tasks.
- Personal relationships also benefit, as the absence of digital distractions allows for deeper, more meaningful interactions.
- Being fully present is a rare gift that strengthens connections and fosters empathy.
- Creating a balanced digital routine involves practical steps that integrate wellness into daily life.
- Using apps or phone settings to limit screen time can act as a gentle nudge, reminding you to take breaks and engage with the world around you.
- Consider encouraging family or group digital detox challenges, where everyone commits to unplugging at certain times.

The journey towards digital balance is about finding what works for you and creating a lifestyle that integrates technology as a tool rather than letting it dominate your existence. As you travel this path, remember that the most meaningful moments often happen offline, in spaces where laughter echoes, conversations deepen, and memories are made.

What ideas do you have that will help you find a healthy digital balance

_____

_____

_____

_____

_____

_____

_____

_____

_____

_____

_____

_____

_____

_____

_____

_____

_____

Digital Detox: Reclaiming Your Offline Life

Successfully planning a digital detox requires setting clear goals and intentions.
- Why are you taking this break, and what do you hope to achieve
- Identifying your reasons helps clarify your purpose, making the detox more meaningful.
- It's also crucial to recognize triggers for excessive device use.
- Are there specific apps or notifications that pull you in?

By understanding these triggers, you can create strategies to manage them, such as turning off notifications or limiting app usage during detox.

These steps lay the groundwork for a successful digital detox, ensuring you can fully embrace the break without unnecessary distractions.

Make some notes here about your goals and intentions

_____

_____

_____

_____

_____

_____

_____

_____

_____

_____

_____

_____

_____

_____

Space for Doodles

The emotional benefits of disconnecting are profound. Without the constant flood of information and connectivity, you can begin to grow increased mindfulness and presence. As your mind quiets, you may find engaging with your thoughts and surroundings easier, fostering a sense of calm and clarity.

To maximize your time offline, consider activities that promote connection without screens.
- Nature walks and outdoor adventures are excellent ways to engage with the world and nurture your well-being.
- Arts and crafts or journaling sessions provide another avenue for expression and creativity.

Make some notes here about offline activities you enjoy

_____

_____

_____

_____

_____

_____

_____

_____

_____

_____

_____

_____

After completing a digital detox, take time to think about the experience. Journaling about your thoughts and feelings during the detox can reveal valuable insights into your relationship with technology.

- What did you find challenging, and what surprised you?
- How did the absence of screens affect your mood and interactions?
- How can these reflections guide you in setting new digital habits that support a healthier balance between online and offline life?

As you explore the benefits of a digital detox, consider how these practices might influence your relationship with technology moving forward. Embracing digital balance is about reclaiming control, where technology is a tool rather than a tether.

Make some notes here about your experience

_____

_____

_____

_____

_____

_____

_____

_____

_____

_____

_____

_____

Space for doodles

Chapter 5:
Enhancing Communication Skills

Expressing emotions clearly doesn't always come naturally. Developing clear expression skills requires practice and feedback. Emotion expression journals offer a safe space to explore and articulate your feelings. Set aside time each day to write about your emotions, using "I feel" statements to describe your experiences. Over time, this practice enhances self-awareness and hones your ability to express emotions effectively.

As you explore these techniques, remember that clear expression is valuable in your communication toolkit. It empowers you to connect with others on a deeper level, fostering understanding and empathy. By clearly speaking your truth, you invite others to do the same, creating a cycle of openness and authenticity in your relationships.

Emotion Expression Journaling Prompt
- Write about a recent situation that stirred strong emotions.
    - Use "I feel" statements to describe your emotions.
    - Think about how clearly expressing these feelings could have improved the situation.

Use this space to think about a recent situation

_____

_____

_____

_____

Space for Doodles

5.1 Conflict Resolution: Turning Disagreements into Dialogue

The techniques for resolving conflicts are as varied as the conflicts themselves, but specific strategies prove consistently helpful. Active listening and validation are cornerstones of this process. When you truly listen to someone, you show them their perspective is valued, even if you disagree. This validation opens the door for honest communication and reduces defensiveness. Creating win-win solutions through compromise is another powerful technique. Instead of viewing the conflict as a battle to be won, consider it a puzzle to be solved. You can find outcomes that satisfy all parties involved by identifying shared goals and exploring creative solutions. This mindset fosters cooperation and mutual respect, transforming adversaries into allies.

Empathy plays a crucial role in conflict resolution. By understanding others' perspectives, you ease tensions and pave the way for meaningful dialogue. Techniques for finding common ground are invaluable here. Start by acknowledging the emotions and concerns of others, even if you don't share them. This acknowledgment shows that you respect and are willing to consider their viewpoint. Exercises in perspective-taking can further enhance your ability to empathize. Picture yourself in the other person's position, considering how their background and experiences might shape their perspective. This practice fosters compassion and understanding, allowing you to approach conflicts with an open heart and mind.

Conflict resolution is not about eliminating disagreements but transforming them into opportunities for connection and growth. By approaching conflicts with empathy, open communication, and a willingness to find common ground, you lay the groundwork for stronger relationships and a more harmonious world.

Conflict Resolution Role-Play Scenarios

1. Scenario: Group Project Workload Imbalance
Scenario: Two classmates disagree on how to divide tasks for a group project. One feels overwhelmed with the workload, while the other believes they are pulling their weight.

Objective: Practice active listening and compromise to find a solution that satisfies both parties.

2. Scenario: Friend Group Miscommunication
Scenario: Two friends are upset because one didn't respond to texts about weekend plans. The other feels ignored and left out, while the first says they were overwhelmed and needed space.

Objective: Practice expressing feelings without blaming, and using empathy to understand each other's perspective. Aim to restore trust and clarify expectations around communication.

3. Scenario: Disagreement During a Sports Game

Scenario: During a basketball game in gym class, one student accuses another of not passing the ball and being selfish. The accused student feels unfairly targeted and says they're just trying to help the team win.

Objective: Practice assertive communication and staying calm under pressure. Work on identifying shared goals and using respectful language to resolve misunderstandings.

4. Scenario: Social Media Conflict

Scenario: A teen posts a joke online that another peer finds hurtful. The poster says it was meant to be funny and not personal, but the other person feels embarrassed and disrespected.

Objective: Practice taking accountability, apologizing sincerely, and setting boundaries. Explore how to resolve digital conflicts in a mature and respectful way.

Space for Doodles

5.2 The Language of Emotions: Words Matter

The power of word choice in emotional expression is immense. Positive language can uplift you, while negative language can weigh you down. Language shapes our reality, and the words we choose can either clarify or confuse our emotions with others. This is where the distinction between positive and negative language becomes crucial. Positive expressions build bridges, inviting others into your emotional world. In contrast, negative expressions can create barriers, leading to misunderstandings that might not have been intended.

Creating a nuanced emotional vocabulary enriches your ability to communicate. This richness in language helps you articulate your emotions more accurately. It allows others to relate to and support you better. Encouraging descriptive language fosters a deeper connection with your emotions, helping you manage them more clearly. When you expand your vocabulary, you enhance your emotional intelligence, allowing you to engage with your emotions in a more meaningful way.

The impact of language on relationships is profound. Words can either strengthen bonds or weaken them. When you choose your words with intention, you create a space where empathy and understanding can flourish.

To expand your emotional vocabulary, try exercises designed to enhance your language skills. Create an emotion word bank, collecting words that resonate with your experiences. This collection can serve as a reference, helping you precisely articulate your emotions. Writing exercises focusing on descriptive language can also be beneficial. Take a moment to describe a recent emotional experience in detail, using as many expressive words as possible. Think about how these words capture the essence of your emotions. These activities enhance your vocabulary and deepen your self-awareness, empowering you to express your emotions with authenticity and clarity.

Space for Doodles

Emotion Word Bank Exercise

Create a list of emotion words that resonate with your experiences. Consider words like "elated," "melancholic," "content," or "frustrated."

Think about recent experiences and choose words that capture the depth and nuance of your emotions.

Write in descriptive language about a recent experience

_____

_____

_____

_____

_____

_____

_____

_____

_____

_____

_____

_____

_____

_____

_____

5.3 Nonverbal Nuance: Reading Between the Lines

There is power in nonverbal communication, an unspoken language that reveals more than words ever could. Body language, facial expressions, and tone of voice convey emotions that might not be vocalized. Congruence between verbal and nonverbal cues is crucial; when these signals align, the message is clear and trustworthy. But when they don't, confusion arises.

Interpreting nonverbal cues is an art that can transform how you connect with others. Reading facial expressions is key; a smile might mean happiness, but a tight-lipped one could indicate discomfort. Body language, such as crossed arms or tapping feet, can speak volumes about someone's emotional state. Recognizing tone is equally important; a sharp tone can imply anger, even if the words are neutral. Understanding these signals allows you to handle the situation in a positive way, fostering empathy and connection.

5.4 Role-Play Scenarios: Practice Makes Perfect

You may want to ask an adult to help with some of this; their life experience may help you brainstorm additional situations to role-play, and they can help lead the feedback discussions if needed. Setting clear objectives for each session is essential to create role-playing scenarios that work.

1. Scenario: Awkward Vibes in a Group Project
What's Happening: One person in your group keeps crossing their arms, won't look at anyone, and keeps sighing. It's making the rest of the group feel unsure and uncomfortable.
What to Practice: Picking up on body language that shows someone might be upset, even if they don't say anything out loud.
After-Roleplay Chat:
Facilitator: "What were they doing that made you think something was off?"
Teen(s): Response/discussion
Facilitator: "How did that make you feel? What could you do to check in with someone acting that way?"
Teen(s): Response/discussion

2. Scenario: Joke Gone Wrong
What's Happening: You joke around and lightly bump your friend on the arm, but they don't laugh or smile—they just pull away and go quiet.
What to Practice: Noticing when someone's body language says, "That wasn't funny" or "I didn't like that."
After-Roleplay Chat:
Facilitator: "How could you tell they weren't into the joke?"
Teen(s): Response/discussion

Facilitator: "What's a good way to handle that kind of reaction?"
Teen(s): Response/discussion

3. Scenario: Quiet in a Group Chat

What's Happening: You're in a small group and one person hardly talks, keeps their head down, and looks at the floor. People assume they don't want to help.

What to Practice: Realizing someone might be nervous or shy—not rude or lazy.

After-Roleplay Chat:

Facilitator: "What did you think when they didn't speak much?"
Teen(s): Response/discussion
Facilitator: "What's another reason someone might be quiet? How can you include them without putting them on the spot?"
Teen(s): Response/discussion

4. Scenario: "I'm Fine" But...Not Really

What's Happening: You ask a friend what's wrong, and they say "I'm fine," but their face is tense, arms are crossed, and they won't look at you.

What to Practice: Noticing when someone's words don't match their body language—and how to respond kindly.

After-Roleplay Chat:

Facilitator: "Did their body match what they said?"
Teen(s): Response/discussion
Facilitator: "What's a nice way to show you care when someone says they're okay but doesn't look it?"
Teen(s): Response/discussion

5. Scenario: The New Kid at Lunch

What's Happening: A new student is sitting alone, looking over at your table, kind of fidgeting and not talking to anyone.

What to Practice: Spotting signs that someone wants to be included—and making the first move to help them feel welcome.

After-Roleplay Chat:

Facilitator: "What made you think they wanted to join you?"
Teen(s): Response/discussion
Facilitator: "What could you do to show they're welcome without making it awkward?"
Teen(s): Response/discussion

Chapter 6: Building Resilience and a Growth Mindset

Resilience is the inner strength that helps you bounce back from difficulties, like a bad grade or a sudden change of plans. It's not about avoiding challenges but embracing them and finding ways to grow stronger through them. Resilient individuals possess a unique blend of traits—perseverance, flexibility, and optimism. They understand that setbacks are a part of life and view them as opportunities for personal growth. The importance of resilience cannot be overstated, as it plays a crucial role in personal development, equipping you with the tools to deal with life's ups and downs confidently.

Building resilience is a journey that unfolds over time, shaped by the experiences and lessons learned along the way. As you continue to explore resilience, remember that each challenge is an opportunity to strengthen your inner resolve, guiding you toward a more confident and resilient self.

Resilience-Building Exercise

Problem-Solving Scenario:
- o Think of a recent challenge you experienced.
- o Break the experience down into smaller parts and brainstorm possible solutions for emotion or reaction.
- o Think about the outcomes and what you learned from the experience.

Make some notes here about your experience

_____

_____

_____

Space for Doodles

Embracing Failure: Learning from Setbacks

Reframing failure as an opportunity rather than a defeat can profoundly change how you approach life's challenges - failure is not the opposite of success but a crucial part of it.

Viewing failure positively requires a mindset shift from seeing it as a personal flaw to understanding it as feedback. Each misstep offers valuable insights and lessons that guide you toward improvement. Encouraging this shift involves embracing the idea that failure provides the feedback needed to refine your approach and strategies. Rather than focusing on the embarrassment of a setback, concentrate on what it teaches you and how it can inform your next steps. Doing so transforms failure from a source of shame into a stepping stone toward your goals.

What can you change to help you find success.
- Do you need to be in the presence of different people to succeed, how can you make that happen?
- Is there something you can change about your surroundings to help you be successful?
- Do you need different or more support to find success, how can you build a stronger network?
- What might need to change about where you are at to allow you to find your highest worth?
- Strategies for learning from failure can help you harness its potential.

Begin with reflection exercises that encourage you to identify the lessons found within each setback.
- Consider what went wrong, why it happened, and what you can do differently next time.
- This reflection isn't about dwelling on mistakes but extracting wisdom from them.
- Once you've identified these lessons, use them to set new, informed goals.

This method drives personal growth and ensures that each failure becomes a catalyst for future success. Setting goals based on past experiences creates a cycle of continuous improvement and development.

The emotional impact of failure is undeniable. It can stir feelings of disappointment, frustration, and even self-doubt. However, managing these emotions is crucial for bouncing back stronger. Techniques for handling disappointment include acknowledging your feelings without letting them define you. Allow yourself to feel upset, but set a time limit on how long you'll dwell on these emotions. Then, shift your focus to actionable steps for moving forward. Building resilience against the fear of failure involves growing a mindset that views setbacks as temporary and manageable. By embracing this perspective, you reduce the power of fear and increase your willingness to take risks and pursue your dreams.

Space for Tiny Doodles

Make some notes here about a recent setback/failure you experienced

_____

_____

_____

_____

_____

_____

_____

_____

_____

_____

_____

_____

_____

_____

_____

_____

The Growth Mindset Game: Turning Obstacles into Opportunities

Cultivating a growth mindset involves embracing obstacles or challenges with an open mind. Setting incremental challenges is a powerful technique to encourage skill development.

Start by identifying a skill or area you wish to improve, then break it down into smaller, manageable goals.

- Each small success builds confidence and momentum, creating a sense of progress.
- Emphasizing effort and process over results is equally crucial.
- Focus on the journey of learning rather than the destination, valuing perseverance and dedication.
- Feedback plays a vital role in nurturing a growth mindset.
- Constructive feedback provides insight into areas for improvement, guiding you toward better performance.
- Seek feedback actively from teachers, peers, or mentors, and view it as a tool for growth rather than criticism.
- Apply the feedback by setting specific goals and strategies to address identified weaknesses.
- Practicing self-reflection further enhances learning.
- Take time to evaluate your progress, considering what worked, what didn't, and why.
- Incorporating activities to reinforce growth-oriented thinking is beneficial.
- Try growth mindset journaling, where you document challenges faced, lessons learned, and successes achieved.
- Think about moments of difficulty and note how perseverance led to breakthroughs. These entries remind you of your capacity for growth, motivating you to keep pushing forward.
- Group discussions on overcoming challenges offer another avenue for growth. Share experiences with peers, exchanging insights and strategies. Such conversations provide diverse perspectives, enriching your understanding and encouraging collective learning.

Make some notes here about a recent obstacle you experienced and people you can turn to for feedback

_____

_____

_____

_____

_____

Space for Doodles

The Resilience Journal: Documenting Your Journey

To maintain a resilience journal effectively, consider incorporating daily reflection prompts. These prompts act as gentle nudges, guiding your thoughts and helping you focus on specific areas.

Questions like these can open doors to deeper insights:
- "What challenge did I face today, and how did I handle it?"
- "What am I grateful for right now?"

Setting and tracking personal goals within your journal can be transformative. Outline your aspirations and break them into actionable steps, noting your progress along the way. This structured method keeps you accountable and provides a tangible record of your achievements and milestones, reinforcing your capacity for growth and resilience.

Sample Journal Entry: Reflecting on Overcoming Challenges

"Today was kinda chaotic. We had a group project and everyone was talking over each other—no one could agree on anything. I was stressed out, but I took a breath, listened to what people were actually trying to say, and suggested we just split stuff up based on what we're good at. After that, things started to click. I realized I can actually keep my cool and help pull things together when stuff gets crazy."

The insights gained through resilience journaling are profound. They offer a window into your journey, highlighting moments of growth and transformation. By reflecting on these experiences, you build a deeper understanding of yourself, your values, and your aspirations. This practice nurtures self-compassion, reminding you that progress is a continuous process, not a destination. It allows you to embrace your imperfections, seeing them as opportunities for learning and growth rather than obstacles. As you continue to document your journey, you'll find that each entry, each reflection, is a building block, laying the foundation for a resilient and empowered self.

Consider your own life:
- What challenges have you faced, and how did you respond?
- Are there moments where you found unexpected strength?
- Identifying the strategies that helped you can be empowering.
- Did you seek help, find an outlet, or simply refuse to give up?

Make some notes here about a recent challenge you overcame, use this to start your own Resilience Journal

_____

_____

Tiny space for tiny Doodles

Chapter 7
Real-World Scenarios

For many, school isn't just a place of learning; it's a battleground of stressors that can feel overwhelming. From the pressure of securing top grades to the looming deadlines of assignments, the weight of these challenges can take a toll on both emotional and mental health. Understanding and managing this stress is crucial, not only for academic success but also for overall well-being.

One of the primary sources of stress in school is the pressure from exams and grades. The expectation to perform well can weigh heavily on students, creating anxiety that affects both sleep and concentration. It's not just the exams themselves; the anticipation and fear of not meeting expectations can be paralyzing. Time management adds another layer of complexity. Balancing multiple assignments with personal commitments can often feel like juggling flaming torches. The constant race against deadlines can lead to burnout, affecting mood and academic performance. Recognizing these stressors is the first step in addressing them.

Stress Management Reflection Exercise

Think about a recent school challenge. Identify the primary stressors and consider which strategies from this book might help you manage these pressures.

Write a short plan detailing how you will implement these techniques in your daily routine.

_____

_____

_____

_____

_____

_____

_____

_____

_____

_____

_____

_____

_____

_____

_____

_____

_____

Space for Doodles

7.1 Friendship Drama: Navigating Social Circles

Navigating the intricate web of teenage friendships can feel like walking on a tightrope. One minute, everything is harmonious, and the next, you find yourself tangled in a web of misunderstandings and rumors. These are common sources of drama in social circles, often stemming from miscommunication or a casual remark that spirals out of control. There's the instance when a friend might misinterpret a text message, leading to confusion and, potentially, a rift. Or when a joke, meant to be lighthearted, is taken the wrong way, causing feelings to be hurt. Rumors, too, can spread like wildfire, fueled by snippets of truth mixed with exaggeration, turning minor issues into major conflicts.

Jealousy and competition are other culprits that can disrupt friendships. It's natural to feel envious when a friend excels in an area where you struggle, whether it's academics, sports, or social popularity. However, when left unchecked, jealousy can breed resentment and create distance. This is especially true when friends compare themselves to one another, feeling that they must outdo each other to maintain their self-worth. The resulting competition can erode the foundation of trust and support that genuine friendships are built upon.

Conflict Resolution Checklist
- Identify the core issue causing conflict.
- Come to the conversation with a calm and open mindset.
- Use "I feel" statements to express emotions without blame.
- Listen actively and validate the other person's feelings.
- Set clear boundaries and discuss ways to prevent future conflicts.

Think about a recent conflict you had with someone and use the Conflict Resolution Checklist to process what happened

_____

_____

_____

_____

_____

_____

_____

_____

_____

_____

_____

_____

_____

_____

_____

_____

Space for Doodles

7.2 Family Dynamics: Understanding and Communicating at Home

Family dynamics often present unique challenges, with communication styles being one of the biggest hurdles. Generational differences can create misunderstandings; parents might value direct conversations, while teens may prefer more casual, indirect exchanges. These differences can lead to conflicts over responsibilities and expectations, where what seems reasonable to one generation feels overwhelming to another. For example, parents might expect teens to manage chores and schoolwork effortlessly, not realizing the stress it adds to their already packed schedules.

To bridge these gaps, fostering positive family communication can make a world of difference. Establishing regular family meetings can be a game-changer. These gatherings create a dedicated space for everyone to voice concerns and share updates, fostering a sense of inclusion and cooperation. During these meetings, encouraging the use of "I feel" statements helps family members express emotions without casting blame. Instead of saying, "You never help with the dishes," one might say, "I feel overwhelmed when I have to manage all the chores alone." This simple shift in language can diffuse tension and open the door for constructive dialogue, allowing family members to express themselves honestly while minimizing defensive reactions.

Write down your ideas on how you could improve your communication with family members, what do you think will change?

_____

_____

_____

_____

_____

_____

_____

_____

_____

_____

_____

_____

_____

_____

_____

_____

Space for Doodles

7.3 Sportsmanship: Emotions on the Field

Sports are more than just physical contests; they're an onslaught of emotions that test your courage and your ability to work within a team. The pressure of competition can be intense, with every player striving to outperform the other. Winning brings elation, while losing can sting like a fresh wound. These emotional highs and lows are part of the athletic journey, each game a small-scale version of life's broader challenges. Managing these emotions is key to not just surviving but thriving in sports.

To manage the emotional landscape of sports, athletes need strategies to maintain composure and focus. Visualization exercises can be particularly helpful. Picture yourself scoring a goal or executing a perfect play. This mental rehearsal prepares your mind for success, boosting confidence and reducing anxiety. It's like seeing a map before embarking on a journey; you know the terrain and can confidently travel it. Before a match, breathing techniques such as deep breathing can help calm nerves. Slow, deliberate breaths can slow your heart rate and center your thoughts, allowing you to channel your energy into the game. These techniques enable you to control your physiological responses and focus clearly, even under pressure.

Write down the techniques that work for you. Are there new techniques you have learned about that you think would be beneficial? Track them and your progress towards improved sportsmanship.

_____

_____

_____

_____

_____

_____

_____

_____

_____

7.4 Facing Rejection: Constructive Coping Strategies

Rejection. Just the word itself can sting, bringing with it a flood of emotions that can feel overwhelming.

Reframing rejection as a learning opportunity is a powerful way to shift your perspective. Instead of viewing it as a definitive judgment of your abilities or character, consider it as feedback that guides your growth. This doesn't mean dismissing the disappointment or hurt but rather using it to fuel your determination. Seek feedback wherever possible. Understanding why you didn't achieve your goal can provide valuable insights and help you set new, realistic targets. For instance, if a college application falls short, analyzing areas for improvement can prepare you for future success. Setting new goals based on this feedback turns rejection into a stepping stone rather than a stumbling block, encouraging resilience and perseverance.

Practicing self-compassion is essential in coping with rejection. It's about being gentle with yourself and recognizing that setbacks are a part of life, not a reflection of your worth. Affirmations can play an important role in bolstering self-esteem. Simple phrases like "I am capable" or "I am worthy" repeated regularly can counteract negative self-talk and reinforce a positive self-image. Alongside affirmations, engaging in self-care activities can restore emotional balance. Whether it's taking a long walk, diving into a good book, or spending time with friends, nurturing yourself helps heal the wounds of rejection and renews your sense of well-being.

Rejection is an inevitable part of life, but it doesn't have to define you. You can work through the emotional waves it brings and emerge stronger by approaching it with a growth mindset and self-compassion. These experiences teach resilience, highlighting the importance of perseverance and adaptability in personal and academic pursuits. As you think about these strategies, remember that every setback carries the potential for growth, shaping you into a more resilient and self-assured individual. With each rejection faced and overcome, you build a foundation of strength that prepares you for future challenges, equipping you with the tools to thrive in an ever-changing world.

Write down the coping strategy techniques that work for you. Think about a recent experience of rejection and write down how the experience helped you find strength and resiliency.

_____

_____

_____

_____

_____

_____

_____

_____

_____

_____

_____

_____

_____

_____

_____

_____

_____

Small space for small Doodles

Chapter 8:
Mindfulness and Well-Being Practices

Starting your day with mindfulness can provide a foundation of peace and focus, allowing you to deal with challenges with grace and resilience. Incorporating mindfulness into your morning routine can be a game-changer, offering benefits that ripple through the day.

The intention to begin the day with purpose and presence is at the heart of mindful mornings. It's about creating a routine, prioritizing mental and emotional well-being rather than rushing into the day with a bunch of distractions. The benefits of a mindful morning are multifaceted. By beginning your day with clarity and calm, you set the stage for increased focus and concentration during daily activities. This heightened awareness enhances productivity and builds emotional resilience, equipping you to handle stress and setbacks with a balanced mindset. Practicing mindfulness in the morning serves as a mental reset, clearing the fog of sleep and bringing a fresh perspective to the tasks ahead.

Below is an example of a 10-minute guided meditation before breakfast. This simple practice lets you ease into the day, clearing mental clutter and setting a peaceful tone. By focusing on your breath and gently releasing tension, you relax into a sense of renewal, ready to embrace the day ahead. Another practice to incorporate could be stretching exercises combined with mindful breathing. As you stretch, focus on each movement and breath, feeling the sensations in your body. This prepares your body physically and centers your mind, enhancing your awareness and presence.

Create Your Morning Mindfulness Routine
- Choose a Quiet Space: Find a peaceful spot where you won't be disturbed.
- Set a Timer: Dedicate at least 5-10 minutes to your practice.
- Select a Mindful Activity: Whether meditation, stretching, or affirmations, choose what resonates with you.
- Reflect: After your practice, take a moment to notice how you feel and any changes in your mindset.

Use this space to take notes on what works for you and why, how does each activity make you feel? What is your preference?

_____

_____

_____

_____

_____

_____

_____

_____

_____

_____

_____

_____

_____

_____

_____

_____

_____

8.1 The Body Scan: Tuning into Physical and Emotional Sensations

Practicing the body scan involves a systematic journey through your body, starting from the tips of your toes and working your way up to the crown of your head. Begin by finding a comfortable position, either lying down or sitting, where you won't be disturbed. Close your eyes and take a few deep breaths to center yourself. Focus your attention on your toes, noticing any sensations, whether they are warmth, coolness, or tension. Slowly move your attention upward, part by part, to your ankles, calves, knees, and so on, acknowledging each sensation without judgment. If your mind starts to wander, gently guide it back to the area you're focusing on. This practice is not about emptying your mind but about fostering a curious, non-judgmental awareness of your body's experiences.

The benefits of body scanning extend beyond mere relaxation. It heightens your self-awareness by enhancing your real-time ability to identify stress and tension. By recognizing these sensations, you can address them before they escalate into bigger issues. This awareness also promotes emotional clarity and balance as you learn to connect your physical sensations to your emotions. For instance, you might notice a tightness in your chest during stressful situations, signaling anxiety. Acknowledging this connection can empower you to take steps toward emotional regulation, such as practicing deep breathing or engaging in calming activities.

Body Scan Checklist

- Find a Quiet Space: Choose a comfortable position where you won't be disturbed.
- Focus on Your Breath: Take a few deep breaths to center yourself.
- Scan Your Body: Start from your toes and move upward, noting sensations in each area.
- Acknowledge Without Judgment: Observe sensations without trying to change them.
- Return Focus When Needed: Gently guide your mind back if it starts to wander.

Use this space to take notes on what works for you and why, how does each step make you feel?

_____

_____

_____

_____

_____

_____

Space for Doodles

8.2 Gratitude Journaling: Focusing on the Positive

Gratitude journaling is a powerful tool that prompts you to recognize the abundance in everyday life, shifting your focus from what you lack to what you already have. It's about opening your eyes to small yet important blessings, like a friend's laughter, a warm meal, or the comfort of your home. Regularly acknowledging these positives creates a mindset that appreciates the present, enhancing your happiness and contentment.

To make the most of gratitude journaling, it helps to maintain a consistent practice. Begin by writing three things you're grateful for each day. They don't have to be grand; the simplest joys are often the most profound. Think about why these things matter to you as you write, delving into the feelings they evoke. This reflection deepens your gratitude, transforming it from a fleeting thought to a meaningful acknowledgment. Consider using prompts to guide your journaling. Questions like "What made me smile today?" or "Who am I thankful for?" can inspire thoughtful entries. The key is to make this practice a part of your routine, allowing gratitude to weave through your daily life.

Gratitude Journaling Prompt
Think about today's highlights: Write down three things that brought you joy or comfort. Consider what these moments mean to you and why they matter.

Make some notes here about gratitude you find each day, why are these things important?

_____

_____

_____

_____

_____

_____

_____

_____

_____

_____

_____

_____

_____

_____

_____

_____

Space for Doodles

8.3 The Art of Noticing: Finding Joy in Everyday Moments

This practice of noticing is about cultivating awareness, allowing the present moment to take center stage. It's about finding beauty in the ordinary and joy in the overlooked. When you shift your focus to the details, life unfolds in unexpected, delightful ways, inviting you to engage with the world more deeply.

To practice noticing, start with small, deliberate changes to your daily routine. As you walk to school or work, shift your gaze from your phone to the trees lining the street. Observe the way their leaves flutter in the breeze, the patterns of light and shadow they create. This simple act of observing nature can ground you, pulling you out of your thoughts and into the moment. Similarly, mindful eating can transform a routine meal into an experience. Focus on the flavors, textures, and aromas of each bite. Notice the crunch of a fresh apple or the sweetness of a ripe strawberry. By giving your full attention to these sensations, you deepen your appreciation for the nourishment they provide.

There are practical ways to incorporate noticing into your routine. Start with a simple noticing challenge: commit to identifying five new things each day. These can be as small as the intricate pattern on a leaf or the way sunlight dances on a puddle. This practice trains your mind to seek out novelty and beauty, keeping your perspective fresh and engaged. Another engaging activity is mindful photography. Take a camera or smartphone and capture images of everyday beauty—an interesting shadow, a vibrant flower, a playful interaction between people. This exercise encourages you to look at your environment with an artist's eye, finding inspiration in the mundane.

Noticing Challenge
- Daily Goal: Identify and appreciate five new things each day, whether it's a unique sight, sound, or smell.
- Document Your Discoveries: Write them down or take photos to capture these moments.

Make some notes here about new things you notice each day, what made these things stand out to you?

_____

_____

_____

_____

_____

_____

Space for Doodles

Visualization Techniques: Imagining Your Best Self

To practice effective visualization, begin with guided visualizations focusing on personal development. Find a quiet space where you can relax without interruptions. Close your eyes and take a few deep breaths to center yourself. Imagine a specific goal or aspiration, such as acing your next exam or mastering a musical instrument. Picture every detail of this success—the sights, sounds, and emotions associated with achieving it. Let these sensations fill your mind, creating a vivid mental image that feels tangible and real. Visualization is about seeing and feeling the experience as if it's unfolding in the present moment.

Creating vision boards is another technique that complements visualization. Gather images, words, and symbols that represent your goals and aspirations. Arrange them on a board where you can see them daily, serving as a constant reminder of what you're working towards. Vision boards act as a visual representation of your dreams, reinforcing your commitment to achieving them. They inspire you to take concrete steps toward your goals, turning motivation into action. Regularly engaging with these boards strengthens the connections in your brain associated with your aspirations, making them more attainable and realistic.

The effect of visualization on well-being is profound. Regular practice improves mental clarity and goal orientation as you focus more on what truly matters. Visualization fosters a positive mindset, increasing your motivation and confidence in achieving aspirations. It bridges the gap between where you are and where you want to be, encouraging you to overcome obstacles with determination and resilience. As you visualize success, you begin to grow a belief in your abilities, empowering you to take on challenges with a proactive attitude.

What techniques work best for you? Use this space to write down visualization ideas or thoughts on what to put on a vision board.

_____

_____

_____

_____

_____

_____

_____

Space for Doodles

Chapter 9:
Integrating Emotional Intelligence into Daily Life

Daily EQ habits are the cornerstone of building emotional intelligence over time. Consistency is key—small, regular practices can profoundly affect your emotional well-being. By incorporating these practices, you create a foundation that strengthens your emotional resilience and adaptability, equipping you to handle whatever comes your way with grace and understanding. Emotional intelligence can be nurtured through habits promoting self-awareness, empathy, and emotional regulation, allowing you to better understand yourself and those around you.

One of the most effective ways to build emotional intelligence is through morning reflection on emotional goals. Before you get out of bed, take a few moments to consider what emotional qualities you want to embody that day. Maybe you aim to be more patient, more understanding, or more decisive. Setting these intentions aligns your mindset with your goals, creating a roadmap for your emotional interactions. This practice prepares you for the day ahead and serves as a reminder to check in with yourself, fostering a deeper connection with your emotions. It's about starting your day with purpose, ensuring that your actions and reactions are guided by conscious choice rather than impulsive emotion.

Evening gratitude journaling serves as a powerful bookend to your day. As you wind down in the evening, think about the moments and interactions that brought you joy or taught you something valuable. Write them down, acknowledging the positive aspects of your day, no matter how small. This practice shifts your focus from your challenges to the blessings you encountered, reinforcing a positive outlook. Gratitude journaling enhances your emotional well-being and strengthens your ability to find silver linings in challenging situations. It's a gentle exercise in appreciation that brings a sense of contentment and fulfillment, setting the stage for restful sleep and a positive mindset for the next day.

Daily EQ Habit Tracker

- Morning Reflection: Set your emotional goals for the day; use a prompt like, "Today, I will focus on being [emotion]."
- Evening Gratitude Journaling: Every night, write down three things you are grateful for and why.
- Reminder Setup: Schedule reminders on your phone to prompt these habits.
- Routine Pairing: Decide which existing routine (like breakfast or bedtime) you can pair these habits with.

Use this space to plan out your daily goals, timing and routine pairings.

_____

_____

_____

_____

_____

_____

_____

_____

_____

_____

_____

_____

_____

9.2 Embracing EQ: From Skill to Lifestyle

Imagine emotional intelligence not just as a skill to be learned but as a way of life, permeating every interaction and decision you make. This perspective transforms EQ from a set of practices into a core value that guides how you move through the world. When embraced as a lifestyle, emotional intelligence offers a holistic approach to well-being. It's about viewing EQ not as a final destination to reach but as an ongoing process that continuously enriches your life. By adopting this mindset, you open yourself to the vast benefits that come from living with emotional awareness and empathy at the forefront of your actions. This lifestyle choice affects everything, from how you handle personal relationships to how you tackle challenges at school or work.

Living an EQ centered life involves practicing mindfulness in all your interactions. Mindfulness in this case is about paying attention to the present moment without judgment. It means listening actively when others speak, acknowledging your emotions as they arise, and responding with intention rather than reacting out of habit. This method fosters deeper connections with others and a greater understanding of oneself. By being mindful, you create space for empathy and compassion, both toward yourself and those around you. This strengthens your relationships and builds a foundation of mutual respect and understanding. As you engage with others, whether it's a conversation with a friend or a group project at school, your mindful presence can transform ordinary interactions into meaningful exchanges.

Continuously seeking opportunities for emotional growth and learning is another key aspect of integrating EQ into your lifestyle. This means being open to feedback and embracing new experiences that challenge your emotional understanding. It involves stepping out of your comfort zone to engage with diverse perspectives and learning from those interactions. By actively pursuing emotional growth, you enhance your ability to adapt to changing circumstances and deal with life's complexities with resilience. This continual learning process enriches your life, allowing you to thrive both personally and professionally. Whether it's reading books on emotional intelligence, attending workshops, or simply reflecting on your experiences, each step toward growth adds depth to your emotional capabilities.

The long-term benefits of adopting an EQ lifestyle are profound. It leads to enhanced personal and professional relationships, as empathy and understanding become the norm in your interactions. These qualities foster environments of trust and collaboration, which are essential for success in any setting. Moreover, an EQ focused lifestyle equips you with greater adaptability and resilience. When faced with challenges, you draw on your emotional intelligence to find solutions, turning obstacles into opportunities for growth. This resilience benefits you and inspires those around you, creating a ripple effect of positivity and progress. As you work through life's ups and downs, your EQ serves as a compass, guiding you toward fulfillment and balance.

Emotional intelligence can be woven into the fabric of everyday life, offering a pathway to deeper connections and personal growth. As you move forward, consider how you can integrate these insights into your daily routine, making EQ a guiding principle in all you do.

Conclusion

The journey doesn't end here. Emotional intelligence is a lifelong pursuit, a daily practice that requires commitment and dedication. I encourage you to integrate the habits and techniques we've discussed into your daily routine. Take a moment each morning to set your emotional intentions for the day. Practice mindfulness in your interactions, listening actively and responding with empathy. Keep a gratitude journal, reflecting on the positive moments and lessons learned. These small, consistent actions will compound over time, strengthening your EQ muscles and transforming how you engage with the world.

As you continue on this path, celebrate the progress you've made. Recognize the courage it takes to look inward, to confront your emotions, and to choose growth. You've taken the first steps in unlocking your EQ abilities, and that is something to be proud of. Share your experiences with your peers, inspire them with your example, and foster a community that values emotional intelligence. Together, you have the power to create a ripple effect of positive change, one interaction at a time.

Remember, the journey of emotional intelligence is never truly finished. There is always more to learn and more room for growth. Seek resources that deepen your understanding, whether books, workshops, or online courses. Embrace the challenges that come your way as opportunities to flex your EQ muscles and discover new strengths within yourself.

As we conclude this journal, I leave you with an empowering message: your emotions are not your weakness; they are your greatest strength. By embracing your emotional intelligence, you unlock a world of possibility. You become the architect of your own happiness, the navigator of your own destiny. With EQ as your compass, you have the power to create a life filled with meaningful connections, personal growth, and boundless potential.

Thank you for embarking on this journey with me. Your commitment to personal growth and emotional development is a testament to your strength and courage. As you continue to work through the complexities of adolescence and beyond, remember that your emotional intelligence is your greatest ally. Embrace it, nurture it, and watch as it transforms your world in ways you never thought possible.

References

5 Self-Awareness Activities for Adolescents https://www.spokaneimagine.com/mental-health-blog/5-self-awareness-activities-for-adolescents/

Here's How Journaling Can Benefit Teens https://paradigmtreatment.com/journaling-benefit-teens/

Mind-body therapies for resilience in adolescents https://www.sciencedirect.com/science/article/abs/pii/S016383432400183X

The neurobiology of the emotional adolescent https://pmc.ncbi.nlm.nih.gov/articles/PMC5074886/

Relaxation Exercises: Breathing Basics (for Teens) https://kidshealth.org/en/teens/relax-breathing.html

Mindfulness for Teens: Benefits and Practice Tips https://psychcentral.com/health/the-benefits-of-mindfulness-meditation-for-teens

CBT for Teens: Helping to Reframe Negative Thoughts https://teenbraintrust.com/cognitive-reframing-a-great-tool-for-parents-teens/

The power of forgiveness https://www.health.harvard.edu/mind-and-mood/the-power-of-forgiveness

40 Empathy Activities & Worksheets for Students & Adults https://positivepsychology.com/kindness-activities-empathy-worksheets/

How Empathy Maps Can Help Teachers Connect With ... https://www.edutopia.org/article/how-simple-visual-tool-can-help-teachers-connect-students/

Active listening with pre-teens and teenagers https://raisingchildren.net.au/pre-teens/communicating-relationships/communicating/active-listening

9 Ways to Embrace Altruism (and Why It Matters) - Personal Growth - eNotAlone https://www.enotalone.com/article/personal-growth/9-ways-to-embrace-altruism-and-why-it-matters-r14063/

Why Teaching Kindness in Schools Is Essential to Reduce ... https://www.edutopia.org/blog/teaching-kindness-essential-reduce-bullying-lisa-currie

How Using Social Media Affects Teenagers https://childmind.org/article/how-using-social-media-affects-teenagers/

Cyber-kindness: Spreading kindness in cyberspace https://mprcenter.org/review/cyber-kindness-spreading-kindness-in-cyberspace/

Digital Boundaries For Generation Z - Understanding Teenagers https://understandingteenagers.com.au/digital-boundaries-for-generation-z/

Digital Detox for Teens - Eva Carlston Academy Blog https://evacarlston.com/the-importance-of-digital-detox-how-screen-time-affects-mood-and-mental-health/

3 ways you can help your teen express emotions - Unicef https://www.unicef.org/parenting/mental-health/3-ways-help-teens-express-emotions#:~:text=There%20are%20many%20healthy%20ways,that%20expresses%20how%20they%20feel.

Youth Conflict Resolution Techniques + Life Skills https://elcentronc.org/advocacy/youth-conflict-resolution-techniques-life-skills-processing-conflict-during-a-crisis/

Why the Vocabulary of Emotions is Critical to ... - Presence https://presence.com/insights/why-the-vocabulary-of-emotions-is-critical-to-emotional-intelligence/

89

Unlocking the Power of Nonverbal Communication Skills in ... https://everydayspeech.com/blog-posts/general/unlocking-the-power-of-nonverbal-communication-skills-in-elementary-students-a-social-emotional-learning-perspective/

How to Build Resilience in Children and Teens https://biglifejournal.com/blogs/blog/how-to-build-resilience-children-teens?srsltid=AfmBOoodT_1xW9yVfehf2dK2f8fYAt925EKQXsVAnyqlGtPPjt4tBgCV

Famous Failures: 23 Stories to Inspire You to Succeed https://www.bradaronson.com/famous-failures/

The Growth Mindset Workbook for Teens https://www.socialworkerstoolbox.com/the-growth-mindset-workbook-for-teens/

5 Ways Journaling Can Build Your Resilience - Michelle Pearce https://drmichellepearce.medium.com/5-ways-journaling-can-build-your-resilience-5b80a3ba7966

Top 10 Stress Management Techniques for Students https://www.verywellmind.com/top-school-stress-relievers-for-students-3145179

A parent's guide to handling friendship drama | HealthyU https://blog.erlanger.org/2020/01/27/friendship-drama/#:~:text=Let%20your%20child%2Fteen%20fix%20the%20problem.:text=But%20most%20normal%20friendship%20drama,solve%20it%20him%20or%20herself.

9 Family Therapy Activities to Improve Communication https://overcomewithus.com/parenting/9-family-therapy-activities-to-improve-communication

How to Teach Children to Control Emotions in Sports https://www.teamsnap.com/blog/general-sports/how-to-teach-children-to-control-their-emotions-in-youth-sports

How to Develop a Morning Routine (Teens) (with Pictures) https://www.wikihow.com/Develop-a-Morning-Routine-(Teens)

Body Scan Meditation: Benefits and How to Do It https://www.healthline.com/health/body-scan-meditation

A Brief Gratitude Writing Intervention Decreased Stress and ... https://pmc.ncbi.nlm.nih.gov/articles/PMC8867461/#:~:text=Individuals%20with%20higher%20levels%20of,et%20al.%2C%202015%3B%20Wood

Visualization And Guided Imagery Techniques For Stress ... https://www.mentalhealth.com/library/visualization-and-guided-imagery-for-stress-reduction

11 tips for communicating with your teen https://www.unicef.org/parenting/child-care/11-tips-communicating-your-teen

An Introduction to Emotion Coaching https://www.gottman.com/blog/an-introduction-to-emotion-coaching/

Setting healthy boundaries with your teenager https://parents.au.reachout.com/parenting-skills/building-trust/setting-healthy-boundaries-with-your-teenager

Create a Teen Behavior Contract https://parentandteen.com/discipline-adolescent-responsibility-contract/

10 Emotional Intelligence Habits You Can Start Today https://www.vmapsych.com/resources/10-emotional-intelligence-habits-you-can-start-today

Emotional Intelligence From a Teenage Perspective ... https://www.youtube.com/watch?v=MbmLNr89L-A

The Importance of Emotional Intelligence (Incl. Quotes) https://positivepsychology.com/importance-of-emotional-intelligence/

Mindfulness exercises https://www.mayoclinic.org/healthy-lifestyle/consumer-health/in-depth/mindfulness-exercises/art-20046356

www.ingramcontent.com/pod-product-compliance
Lightning Source LLC
Chambersburg PA
CBHW081004140626
46546CB00019B/3395